Identity Confusion of the Gender Type, "The Way Out"

by
Arthur (Art) Woods

DORRANCE
PUBLISHING CO
EST. 1920
PITTSBURGH, PENNSYLVANIA 15238

Dorrance Publishing Co
585 Alpha Drive
Suite 103
Pittsburgh, PA 15238
Visit our website at www.dorrancebookstore.com

ISBN: 979-8-8852-7194-3
eISBN: 979-8-8852-7650-4

CONTENTS

INTRODUCTION

Let me start by saying that the DEVIL is a liar. (John 8:44):"When he speaks a lie, he speaks of his own: for he is a liar and the father of it." Would you agree that this is true? First, we must agree that there is a Devil, right? The Bible tells us that Satan rebelled against God and was thrown out of heaven. Notice the word "rebelled." The Devil's way is rebellion against God. It always has been and always will be. His nature cannot and will not change.

If you haven't figured it out, I am writing from a Christian standpoint. My reference and foundation is the Bible and what it teaches. (2 Timothy 3:16-17): "All scripture is given by inspiration of God, and is profitable for doctrine, for reproof, or correction, for instruction in righteousness: That the man of God may be perfect, thoroughly furnished unto all good works." This is the perspective of truth that I will bring forth of my effort to portray God's view as it relates to homosexuality, bisexuality, transgender and other gender-related issues.

Homosexuality specifically is identified as a perversion in the Bible. See the attached appendix for some scriptures supporting this.

* * * *

This subject has become a very heated subject in our society. Recent years has even brought about legislation that has legalized gay marriage. Political parties, families and coworkers have fought many a passionate argument battles over this subject.

The Bible tells us that God created male and female. (Gen. 1:27): "So, God created man in his own image, in the image of God created he him: male and female." (Genesis 2:24) says: "Therefore, shall a man leave his father and his mother, and shall cleave unto his WIFE: and they shall be one flesh." This is telling me that marriage is between a man and a woman.

Let me say here that I realize that many people are not Christians. You may even be one. Non-Christians (unbelievers) have no knowledge or understanding of the Bible or the ways of God. I cannot convince an unbeliever that homosexuality is wrong. The Bible says that the eyes of their understanding are not opened. (Ephesians 1:18) reads: "The eyes of your understanding being enlightened; that ye may know what is the hope of His calling, and what the riches of the glory of His inheritance in the saints." (John 3:3): "Jesus answered and said unto him, Verily, verily, I say unto thee, except a man be born again, he cannot see the kingdom of God."

If YOU or someone you know claims to be a Christian and is accepting of gay marriage, homosexuality or other sexual behaviors other than heterosexuality behaviors/marriage, I propose that you/they are either delusional, confused, misinformed and for sure do not know what the scriptures say about this issue. Personally, I find it hard to believe how a "Christian" can support a gay lifestyle and/or gay marriage. So, please give me some time to share how God has enlightened me on my journey.

Chapter 1
Truth or Consequences

Now before you call me some sort of bigot or hater or something, I want to tell you that I have had personal firsthand experience. I have experienced the saving, healing, changing and transforming life of Christ. I have been born again! He has changed me from a sexually confused and same-sex male-attracted person to someone who no longer identifies as such.

Let me start by saying that most would agree that those who have same-sex or other non-heterosexual identifications feel that they were born that way or that they have no control over this. Some accept this and live an open gay lifestyle and others live in secrecy. But I think at some point all must wonder WHY or HOW or WHAT makes one feel something different than being heterosexual.

No matter what your stance is on this issue, we must start at the point of view above. It usually starts early as feeling "different" than others. Yes, there are exceptions and sometimes these attractions do not present themselves until later in life. No person's life experience is the same as another. That's not my point.

What is your position on this issue? So, the question I want to pose to you is, why do you believe that? What belief system or experience are you operating out of? Where did you come up with your perspective on sexual orientations/gender identities, etc.?

I think these are valid questions to consider, propose, explore and possibly even challenge.

But why would you or I want to challenge what we or someone else believes? Why can't I/they believe as we want to and just be left alone? Why can't people just accept homosexuality and other non-heterosexual identities as normal for some? Yet at the other extreme, why can't people just believe that it's not normal for any? Who is right?

Society at present is more accepting of homosexuality than ever, and in fact federal law has decreed that gay marriage is legal and discrimination against sexual orientation, etc., is illegal. So there, that's all we need, right? I beg to differ. Societal morals can and do change. This is the biggest problem in our country currently. Left vs. Right, Liberal vs. Conservative, Pro-Abortion vs. Anti-Abortion, Pro-Gay rights vs. not. Get the picture? There are at least two sides to morality with varying degrees in between.

So which side is right or best or the one we should pick to follow or support? What is the standard if any to choose? Is there anything else besides the "law of the land"? I say there is. For me it is the BIBLE. Again, I am a born-again Christian of some 40 years. This is my perspective and approach to this issue. (John 3:5) states: "Jesus answered, Verily, verily, I say unto thee, except a man be born of water and of the Spirit, he cannot enter into the kingdom of God." So, for me the Spirit of God and the Word of God has become my standard and guide to live my life by. This is my belief. Even if it goes against my own thoughts, hurts or ruffles my feathers. What about you? Where do you stand not only on issues of sexuality but overall? Are you a believer (in Christ and the Bible) or are you not? For me, these are the two sides from which all morality springs (Believers and Non-believers). There is no grey area.

But are there Christians who do immoral things? YES. Are there non-Christians that do moral things? YES, of course. Are there

Christians who believe homosexuality is okay? Yes. Are there non-Christians who believe homosexuality is wrong? Yes, again. Why such differing of opinions? So how can we determine which is better or okay or right or acceptable? We have so much confusion and variation regarding this position; how can there possibly be a right position or answer to this controversial topic? What is the truth?

Chapter 2
The Bible

As a Christian I believe God's WORD is inspired and indicates God's true position about morality and life, including sexuality. PERIOD. I don't have an alternative view or position.

My position comes from some 40 years of personal spiritual experience with following God and His word. Am I perfect and do I know it all? Ya right, don't even go there. I am a man who has had his sins forgiven, but still struggles with fighting the sin that so easily wants to beset me. (Hebrews 12:1): "Wherefore we also are compassed about with so great a cloud of witnesses, let us lay aside every weight, and the sin which doth so easily beset us, and let us run with patience the race that is set before us."

Like every other human, I have fallen short of the ways of God. (Romans 3:23) says: "For all have sinned and come short of the glory of God." We are born in a sinful state and live in a fallen world, beset by sin, and struggle daily with the fallen nature of man. Every person, whether they identify as heterosexual, homosexual or otherwise, must be saved, we're all SINNERS. Homosexuality does not send you to hell, but not being saved through Jesus Christ does! Nor does being a heterosexual save you from hell. Only Jesus Christ can save us from sin and hell, regardless of our sexuality preferences and identifications. You don't change your sexuality to come to Christ, you accept him as your Lord and what He teaches as truth and then He does the rest. One of the defensive responses I hear a lot is that God is a God of love, and we just need to love the homosexual and DON'T JUDGE THEM! I agree. God loves everyone. SO much so that He sent His son Jesus Christ to die for our sins and to bring us into His Kingdom. Therefore, we must accept the finished work of Christ at the cross AND believe the written WORD of God, the Bible. God wants us to accept His love and forgiveness. It's really that simple. Either you do or you don't. If you do, then we start this wonderful journey of being accepted into his family and identifying as a Christian. If not, then, well….

The salvation that God provides is free. What we do with it after we are exposed to it is up to us. The Holy Spirit, the third person of the HOLY Trinity (Father, Son and Holy Spirit), is the one who brings truth as well as both comfort and conviction of sins. How much we allow Him to work in our lives is up to us. (Philippians 2:12) states: "Therefore, my beloved, as ye have always obeyed, not as in my presence only, but now more in my absence, work out your OWN salvation with fear and trembling."

By the grace of God, I have chosen to be committed to following JESUS and His Word. The Bible has many references to homosexuality, and they are not positive. Both New and Old testaments condemn this behavior as sinful and a perversion and not acceptable in the eyes of God. It's in the BIBLE! Therefore, that's what I consider to be the truth. Not much room for debating the BIBLE!

The problem is whether a person <u>decides to believe, obey and live by what the Bible teaches</u>. THIS IS THE BOTTOM LINE, FOLKS! God is God. We are not. We have the choice to believe HIM or another perspective—a lie (ours or society's). As complicated as it is, it is really that simple.

This puts things into perspective. From a Biblical point of view, then, homosexuality is wrong and considered sinful behavior and so if we claim Christ as our Savior, we can't have a differing belief as our truth and expect that it is okay. Can we? In reality we make our differing position an "idol" and we are rebelling against what God has established as His truth. It's deception at its worst! If we willfully oppose God, then we come out from under His blessings and covering of protection.

Chapter 3
Contemplation Time

So now having read this book so far, what do you say? What are your thoughts? Does it challenge anything you believe, or has it made you rethink things? Angry? Confused? Are you still holding to a differing belief? Why or why not? Just where do you stand on this position? And where do you stand with God? These are questions we must ask ourselves if we really want to find truth.

If you do not know Jesus as the Christ (Savior and LORD) of your life, then you are not bound to change your belief or explore any further. I fully understand that you may feel justified to believe what you do about homosexuality. I cannot change your mind. You cannot understand Biblical perspectives if you don't believe that God exists or that He loves you and sent Jesus His Son to die for your sins.

However, if you'd like to change that, then please REPEAT this prayer after me: "Dear Jesus, I confess that I am a sinner and that I have been living my life without you. I need you and want you to save me from my sins and the lifestyle I am living. I accept your free gift of salvation. I believe you took my sins on the cross and now I am saved by your grace. Amen."

So why am I writing this book? Well, it's simple. I am someone who has struggled with sexual identity and same-sex attractions and behaviors. No, I never lived an openly gay or alternative lifestyle, but rather lived a closet life, a life of confusion, and was drawn that way and was not secure at all in who I was.

I'm not just some Bible thumper who is trying to club you over the head to believe like I do. Rather I am a man who was very much lost and in a very bad place of darkness before Jesus Christ came into his life and hit the restart button. He can do the same for you and others. Change didn't happen overnight either. WOW. I look back at how I was bound in pornography, lust, fear, rejection, low self-esteem, drugs, alcohol, and experienced a divorce. I was just troubled in general. Maybe you can relate, maybe not.

I realize not everyone who identifies as homosexual, bisexual, etc., or promotes this as a viable lifestyle was or is in the pit of darkness like I was, but the Bible says that "For all have sinned, and come short of the glory of God" (Romans 3:23). So that tells me that we all need God to save us out of darkness into the light of his Son Jesus Christ. This is being called "born again," which I referred to earlier. I went to Sunday School as a child. Heard about and believed that Jesus was real (in my head), but never had a personal experience of salvation and knowledge of His saving grace until I hit rock bottom as a young adult. Guess I was hardheaded or something.

In 2023 I'll be 68 years old. I've been around the block a few times. I'm not an expert or Bible theologian, but I know what it says about this topic! I wasn't raised in an era that was as accepting of homosexuality as today, but that really doesn't matter. I'm just a man who God touched and called to follow and serve Him. I am a Christian. And now Jesus wants me to share my story and His perspective on homosexuality and other perversions. Believe me when I tell you that this is the last thing that I wanted to do. I fought God and ran from this for several years. Pride, fear, shame, guilt, insecurity and rejection have tried to hold me back. What would people think? It is so personal. But God is stronger than all this and is gracing me with the ability to write this book.

Chapter 4
Testimonial

My story is that JESUS has changed my life! He is real and alive, having been resurrected from the grave just like the Bible says. He now lives in my heart and is the most major influence in my life. He loves me, saved me, forgives me when I sin and shows me the truth of the Bible and how to apply it to my life.

How do I convince you that homosexuality or other gender-related types are not God's plan for you, your loved one, your friend, or anyone else? How do I convince you that gay marriage is unacceptable to support as a Christian?

I don't believe I can, but I do believe that if you honestly and truly open your heart to feel the heartbeat of God the Father, the Spirit of God can and will open your eyes to the truth of His WORD, the Bible. (I John 8:32): "And ye shall know the truth, and the truth shall make you free." The answers are found in the Bible, if one cares to "REALLY" find out the truth about homosexuality as perversion. This is my point here. The problem is that many people don't want to know anything other than what they were told or believe themselves. Let's just stick our heads in the sand or ignore it or go along with the worldly crowd.

Listen: When I got saved, I did not change in preference from homosexual to heterosexual tendencies overnight. WRONG! God did not work some miraculous gender sexuality identity change in me. No way. Not even close. But WHY? I've asked Him that many times.

There is a scripture in the Bible that has ministered to me over the years as I struggle to accept God's way vs. mine. And that is really what this is all about. My way, another way, the homosexual way vs. God's way. The scripture is (2 Corinthians 12:9): "My grace is sufficient for you, for my power is made perfect in weakness...." WEAKNESS. I sometimes detest that word. It means I don't have control over things, including myself. And I must confess I like control. I'm sure you don't, though, huh?

When I gave my life to Jesus, as we say, that included all my life. But the truth of the matter is that some of my life didn't then and sometimes still now does not line up with the truth, strength or power of God. That's why I and you need God in our lives. We don't have the answers within our own strength, power or ability to change ourselves to line up with God's WORD. God knows I've tried. I bet you have too! I have always failed in my efforts to live up to His standard. Heartbreaking, so disappointing, isn't it? That's why we must allow Jesus to be our saving standard. He does the work in us. He does the work of transforming us from glory to glory. (2 Corinthians 3:18) says: "But we all, with open face beholding as in a glass the glory of the Lord, <u>are CHANGED</u> into the same image from glory to glory, even as by the Spirit of the Lord" (emphasis mine). God is the one who accepts and loves us as we are, but also works in us to become made into the image of His Son Jesus. We are a work in progress. Although we are saved from hell to heaven, we are still being purified and cleansed. He does not approve of what He calls sin.

The process of what we Christians call "sanctification" is a process of being changed little by little in our souls. Souls being our mind, will and emotions. This is where the concept of sexuality is located. Let's be honest. You are born either parts associated with male or female in gender. These are the only two genders there are. We read in Genesis of the account of Adam and Eve, man and woman, both heterosexuals. God does not form any of us in our mother's womb as homosexual, bisexual, lesbian, transgender, etc.

David in (Psalms 139:14) said: "I will praise thee, for I am fearfully and wonderfully made...," and if you know anything about David's story, he messed up majorly more than once. Yet God forgave and used Him for His glory.

However, I do believe we can be born with these tendencies, not because we are CREATED this way, but rather because of the sinfulness that is in our bloodlines and inherited. Curses, faults, iniquities, transgressions and sins of the past come through inheritance from our ancestors. It's not much different than a family that has a particular disease or sinful weakness that plagues them for many generations.

WE are three-part beings: BODY, SOUL and SPIRIT. Our spirits ARE SAVED into the kingdom of heaven, delivered from eternal damnation, but our souls are being sanctified (cleansed) as we go. And it is this process of change allowing the Holy Spirit of God to touch our souls and transform our souls (minds, wills and emotions) from what we are to what He would have for us to be. It's amazing what God can do!

This is where my story may differ from others. I am nobody special. But God lovingly set me apart for His will and work as I have allowed Him to. It can happen to you too. It is not easy, but if we want to please Him and do His will, we must submit to His Spirit and Word. If we choose to not cooperate, God who is a loving Father will not force us to comply. He'll let us run, rebel and go against Him if we want to. The choice is ours. But if we make the choice that lines up with Him and His word, then He works to change us for His glory and use. He then places his approval and blessing and anointing upon us. He wants us to help others.

I am not the person I was when I was saved in my late 20s. I'm not even the person I was a few months ago! Really, I would not have been able or willing to be writing this book then. This is the wonder of a personal relationship with Jesus. I go to Him daily. It might be regarding frustrations, anger, unforgiveness, fear, insecurities, faults, lust, lies of the enemy of God who tries to make me believe something other than the TRUTH. I stand on His Word, I even preach his Word (I'm a leader of a small home fellowship), but I am honest with Him about me and what I'm dealing with on the inside. I am a very, very emotional person. Nothing wrong with that as long as my emotions don't rule me. That's a weakness I must bring to Him.

I can't tell you the hours of literally crying out to God to change me and how I see and feel about myself. We have to deal with the reality of what we feel and believe, no matter if it's the truth or not. Even though I know what God's word says, it does not mean that I naturally line up with it in mind, will and emotions/feelings.

However, I have told God I want His will over mine even if it goes against everything that screams within me! And it does at times. Often, it feels like I am dying to what I feel or think! And that is what it means to follow Jesus. Paul says, "I die daily" (1 Corinthians 15:31). My flesh, my soul (mind will and emotions) wars against the things of God. (Galatians 5:17) says: "For the flesh lusts against the Spirit, and the Spirit against the flesh: and these are contrary the one to the other: so that ye cannot do the things that you wish." This means dying to any sexual desires or affections that do not line up with God. Likewise loving the unlovable, forgiving those who we feel don't deserve it, controlling our mouth and emotions, etc.

The Devil does not want us to live holy, pure or sanctified lives. God does. This, however, is not possible without the power of the Holy Spirit. Listen to what it says in the book of (Acts 1:8): "But you shall receive power, that after the Holy Ghost is come upon you: that you shall be witnesses unto me both in Jerusalem, and in all

Judea, and in Samaria, an unto the uttermost part of the earth."

So, the enemy, Satan/the Devil, fights our progress and God's plan to change us. He doesn't want us to live lives that bring glory to God. So, our minds must be renewed in the word of God. (Ephesians 5:26):"That he might sanctify and cleanse it with the washing of water by the word." Jesus lives in and is the Word. (John 1:1-3): "In the beginning was the Word, and the Word was with God, and the Word was God. The same was in the beginning with God. All things were made by Him, and without Him was not anything made that was made." It is a mystery of sort, but it is a reality when He speaks to us through His word. And He does if we seek him with our whole heart. (Jeremiah 29:13):"And you will seek Me and find Me when you search for Me with all your heart."

Several months ago, while praying I had sort of a vision. I saw my two legs, one blue and one pink. Then they turned into both being blue. I believe it was God showing me that He was completing the process of me being made whole as a man. It greatly encouraged me, and I have looked at myself differently ever since. Just one of God's blessings along my journey. Neat, huh?

Chapter 5
Suffering Well

Nobody including me likes to suffer or accept suffering as part of life. Especially after we surrender our lives to Jesus. It seems unfair that we as God's children should still suffer. But the truth of the matter is that we still live in a broken, sinful world that is influenced by the prince of darkness (Satan, the Devil). He does not have more power than God, but he has influence on man especially where there has not been grace, faith and/or repentance appropriated. I have learned so much about the sins that were passed down from my ancestors. We have no idea what some of the people in past generations were involved in which we spiritually inherited, and which affects us! We all have negative spiritual baggage.

One area that I know of is that my family was involved in serving false gods, which is idolatry, which the Bible condemns. God says, "You shall have no other Gods before me" (Exodus 20:3). Specifically, my family was involved in Free Masonry and Eastern Star. Any participation that involves witchcraft, vows, secret societies, activities or rituals dedicated to any other god besides God the Father, Almighty of the Bible, is a false religion. There are lots of books out there on false religion. Including the BIBLE. If you don't accept my analogy, then go educate yourself. That is if you "REALLY" want to know the truth. In short this brought on a spiritual curse to our family involving spiritual bondage to lies, deception and error. This is what perversion is. It perverts the truth and wants us to believe in something else that is a substitute or not condoned by God. It is another "god idol" that takes the place of God Almighty.

The idol of sexual perversion focuses on the same-sex body and/or being with another person sexually of the same sex. It wants to have some part of that which God has reserved for us only to be experienced through a heterosexual union.

This might be a good place to mention that homosexual behavior is not the only sexual sin that God identifies as sin. Fornication (having any sex outside of marriage) and adultery (having sexual relations with someone else, when one or both of you is married to another person). Both are "sin" in the eyes of God.

Our "free" society has made it okay to have sex before and/or outside of marriage and with as many people as we desire. NO limits. Explore, sow some wild oats, enjoy your sexuality, etc. Really? The Bible explicitly says that sex is only to be enjoyed between a married man and woman. I did not set the boundaries. God did.

Again, are we going to line up with God or do our own thing? Just because so many others are doing it does not make it right or acceptable in the eyes of God. <u>This is what living for Jesus really means!</u> It does not mean asking God to forgive you of your sins one time and then living like the rest of the world lives. It's not doing some religious activity as a substitute for living a righteous life of denial. God has called us to a separated life. "Take up your cross and follow me," Jesus said in (Matthew 16:24). This is why and how you leave homosexuality perversion or any other sinful behaviors. You repent and don't do them anymore.

This is where the suffering comes in. It comes in by denying what your flesh wants—those lustful desires you have that are not okay and that you want to do. It's telling yourself that you cannot do certain things and then repenting (or turning from them) and asking God to help you to not do them anymore. We resist the temptations. Do we miss it, give in or fail and sin sometimes, yes? But the important thing is to get up and start doing right again. Eventually we overcome these tendencies as we discipline ourselves and the Holy Spirit strengthens us to live righteously.

We can and do sin in our thoughts as well and we have to ask God to forgive and cleanse us of lustful and/or perverted thoughts. However, we cannot do it on our own. This is the key to Christianity. Christ takes our sins; when we confess them, He forgives us and replaces them with His grace and strength to change our thoughts and behavior. We must replace our thoughts with what God's word says. That's why Christians need to read the Bible and listen to the preaching of the word in a church or elsewhere.

Many have accepted Christ but are living weak, anemic and sinful lives without any testimony for Jesus because they refuse to read and gain spiritual insight, wisdom and knowledge from His Word. Denying yourself hurts, is not fun and does not make sense when you think/feel opposite of what God thinks. That is why we need the mind of Christ to overcome. It's no different than a person overtaken by alcohol or a drug addict having to abstain from those chemicals. You must resist the temptation. Don't tell me that it's not a struggle or that it does not hurt to resist. BUT you find that the more you resist, the less the draw. The stronger you get, the less controlled by these things you are. This is a place to start. Then God takes over.

My life as a born-again Christian has been impacted by Jesus Christ. Not AA or NA or any other manmade support group. I'm not knocking these programs, but Jesus provides a freedom that is more than what they offer. I am no longer a sex addict or pervert. He has changed me from the inside out, but it was Him, not me, that accomplished the work. These other support groups only put a bandage on things, Jesus does open-heart surgery and fixes the problem.

But, for me it has been a long process and involved many things.

He has worked on my masculinity (which was very weak). I walk and talk different these days. I have to laugh. My wife tells me when we were dating that the first time she saw me walking up the sidewalk after she dropped me off at my home one time that I was "swishing all the way up to the front door." And she thought, Lord, what have you gotten me into! Praise God, I don't walk that way anymore, thank the LORD!

God can and does transform us into His image through supernatural means. It is by the Spirit of God that it is done. We need Bible study, prayer, fasting and involvement in a church with leadership that recognizes and flows in the power of the Holy Spirit. A church or group of believers who allows God's Spirit to minister freely and through his ministers as noted in (Ephesians 4:11-12) is a requirement to get set free. "And he gave some, apostles, and some, prophets, and some, evangelists; and some, pastors and teachers; For the perfecting of the saints, for the work of the ministry, for the edifying of the body of Christ." Ministers must be anointed and called by God to teach, preach and lay hands on you for impartation, deliverance and healing. It's unfortunate that some aren't following the Bible and don't even know that God does set the captives free these days. I believe that a homosexual, etc., must have the power of God and the abovementioned things present in their lives for the person to be set free and healed into wholeness. I believe most homosexuals are broken individuals who are looking for love (in all the wrong places) and where Jesus is the REAL answer for their hurting souls. I believe this is why so few actually get set free or believe they can be. But I tell you, it is true. JESUS' love changes lives. Unfortunately, it is because most don't believe in God nor seek God by dedicating themselves to doing whatever it takes that they stay bound in their lifestyle.

Back to suffering.... I have cried (literally) almost daily for years to God, to change me from the inside out. I was so weak, insecure, fearful, anxious, confused. I was sexually molested as a child by another male and exposed to another naked adult man against my wishes. These experiences contributed to my confusion about who I was and what I felt.

I don't really remember the first time I realized I thought I was "different," but it was early on in my childhood. I was what I'd call a "sissy" back then and picked on in school. I hung around girls and was very introverted. I never felt like a "normal" boy. I felt I was in a prison that no one knew about and that it was too terrible to talk about. My family was not an expressive communicative family. Actually, I spent much of my school-aged years at my paternal grandmother's home, who lived just across the yard from our house on the family farm. I felt I was the black sheep of the family. And I knew it. To this day I believe the enemy of my soul targeted me and was trying to take me out because God had plans for me that I knew not of. I developed an obsession looking at other men and their body parts. It started back then with National Geographic magazines. A few naked pictures of natives over in Africa or somewhere. Just enough to get me started.

When older I became involved in pornography. It started before I got saved, but I struggled for several years afterwards until Jesus helped me break free. I was in bondage. I had to take my own steps of denying myself this addiction. God did not do it for me but helped me as I asked Him to do so. I know that porn is prevalent today, even in many Christian men. They have succumbed like I did to trying to get some unmet need addressed. Sexual temptations are real and if left unrestrained will suck you into a world of darkness, bondage, perversion and addictive lust. If you are involved, my advice to you is get out, get out now! Don't play with fire, it is going to burn you.

The Devil comes but to kill, steal and destroy. The trouble is that pornography is so easily available. Just a click away on the computer or phone. You must get sick and tired of being sick and tired! Do something. Confess it and ask Jesus for help. You are not alone. There are ministries and other Christians who can assist you to get free and stay free. Get delivered and set free! It is possible!

SHAME and GUILT were my worst enemies. To this day, I battle these devils who try to intimidate me into believing that I am just a lowlife perverted bum. Unclean thoughts come and the Devil says, "See, you're just the same as you've always been." LIAR. I'm not. Boy, does he try hard. This is where the spiritual battle takes place, in the MIND. This is where we replace our carnal thinking with words from God's word. (Philippians 4:8) says: "Finally, brethren, whatsoever things are true, whatsoever this are honest, whatsoever this are just, whatsoever things are PURE, whatsoever things are lovely, whatsoever things are of good report; if there be any virtue, and if there be any praise, think on these things."

I believe God is calling me to write this book for some of you who just don't know what the truth is and how to appropriate what God has done for you in order to overcome this wicked perversion called homosexuality or other sexual gender-related identity issues being faced. It is rampant in our culture and unfortunately in the Church, if we'd get honest about it. It's nothing new. It's been around as long as recorded time. It's addressed in the Bible as SIN.

However, today we have the gay agenda in the forefront as an acceptable alternative lifestyle to what is the norm. This is the battle that so many are facing. It's so widely accepted and promoted; how can it be wrong? It's on TV. Many homosexuals are so kind and sensitive and don't hurt anyone. That is true. (Contrary to those who militantly march down the street half-naked with their gay flags.) I as well as many others find that very offensive. But there are so many others who are just everyday people who are struggling with the reality of what they are facing. Some just live closet lives, others embrace it and unfortunately have no issue with it, at least it seemingly appears so. They don't even know that Jesus is the answer and that He can and will change them! But it takes faith and a born-again and dedicated spirit-filled life to get free!

I think the main issue here is not whether you identify as homo or heterosexual or anything in between. It is a sin issue in general! People are lost sinners because they don't know God. Not because one is a homosexual, bisexual, etc., etc. As sinners they sin, and since homosexuality is sin, then some people are going to be involved in that sin. If you are not saved, it doesn't matter what sexual preference you practice or identify with or as. Lost is lost, regardless of how you identify sexually.

SO, I guess my bottom line here is, accepting salvation through Jesus Christ. This is what is needed for everyone. Homosexual or not. And then submitting to God by living a life that is in line with the scriptures. If you want to be set free from homosexuality and other sins, you can be, but it is your choice. Personally, for me once I learned what the truth was, it was a no-brainer. No matter how difficult the struggle. God loves me and as my Father only wants the best for me. He is much more loving and ready to forgive than you or I. Why would anyone confronted with the truth of God's love through Jesus Christ reject so great a salvation just because they want to live a life contrary to God's word or choose to not accept a Holy God's way?

Maybe you are not someone who has or is facing this issue yourself? Maybe you know someone else and now want them to know the truth? What do you do? Pray, believe God and if led, share this book. God made a way for me to become whole again, and His heart is to reach others. If this book helps one person see the light of God's love and like me gets changed, it is well worth it to me.

Thank you, Lord, for the privilege of sharing. I pray you use this book to touch the person reading it, in Jesus' name.

Chapter 6
Fathers & Mothers

You don't have to read too many books or articles about sexuality without someone mentioning the role that parenting and nurturing has on a person. Specifically, the overbearing or coddling mother and/or the passive or absent father. I realize that there are many people who seemingly turn out okay, even though they had poor or absent parents. But I think it warrants us looking at what I believe to be a very likely contributor to those of us who have experienced some sort of sexuality confusion and/or perversion.

First of all, a family is best suited to be healthy with two married opposite-sexed parents present. However, that is assuming that those two parents are healthy themselves. Obviously, there are exceptions to the rule here. Many a single mom or even dad have been able to raise children who grew up "normal." Let's go beyond this and look at things from several perspectives to gain some knowledge as to how children are affected by parents.

Mothers are very necessary to provide nurturance, especially in the early years of infancy. Without this there is a greater risk of some sort of problems developing with a child. Likewise, the father is there to be a strength and supporter for the family, a provider if you will. But he also has a role in determining how the family functions and responds to one another, others, problems and crises.

A mother or father who is very weak in the traditional roles, so to speak, runs the risk of negatively affecting the children. If the father is absent, of course we can about imagine the different issues that can arise: rejection, insecurity, fear, poverty, etc. A father's role is to provide security, protection and provision for his household. He is also to be the "spiritual leader." Unfortunately, many a man is not all or sometimes any of these things. What then? Well, then, the child(ren) doesn't develop the normal healthy personalities that God wants them to have.

Bring in any form of abuse, such as physical, domestic, verbal or sexual towards the mother or children, and what do you have? A messed-up kid. Neglect and/or abandonment, likewise, contribute negatively to the children. A person can be absent and yet be around a lot. If that man never had put into the child (for whatever reason) what they needed in order to be a healthy individual, chances are great that they will lack something.

Control and manipulation or abuse are not good traits by which to relate to a spouse or children. God never intended for a man and a woman to mistreat each other. Anger, jealousy, bitterness, unforgiveness, dishonor and belittling someone is the Devil's way of trying to destroy the traditional nuclear family and the individuals in it.

Divorce is one of the most negative things that can happen to a family. Children often are the most negatively scarred. This brings on attachment issues, fear of intimacy, self-rejection, identity confusion, anger, fear and other emotional scars that children often carry through their life. Then if they then get married, continue the ugly cycle of family dysfunction.

Back to the father: He can have addiction problems. A man can be angry and mean. Bad deal. But a man can be passive, detached and distant. Another bad deal. Without God it is nearly impossible for a man to rear children the way God intended. A man must know the love of his heavenly Father to really succeed at fathering a child. There are all levels of love and care that a man can and does provide, but this is in his own limited strength if he does not know Jesus.

Chapter 7
The Mystery of Faith & Spiritual Gifts

I also want to tell you that the Spirit of God can come on us in a greater way than some of you have known or experienced. In the Book of Acts, we learn that God wants to give us spiritual gifts. There is something called speaking in tongues. I speak in tongues. I consider myself a Pentecostal person, one who believes in what happened on the day of Pentecost. This is a mystery. It does not make sense in our brain, but rather only in our spirit man on the inside. This is something that God blessed me with as a new Christian (when I asked Him for it). It is called the baptism of the Holy Spirit. It's in the Bible. It is Christian. It is God. Read (Acts 2:4): "And they were filled with the Holy Ghost, and began to speak with other tongues, as the Spirit gave them utterance."

Are we going to doubt it is a God thing, just because it's foreign to us or we have not experienced it or even that some churches believe this is not for us today? Some even say it is of the Devil. What do you say? And why?

You see, if we seek God's perfect will vs. ours, it opens up a whole new world. A spiritual world of belief in a supernatural God and how His Kingdom works. Understanding and accepting what He has established as truth and righteousness. This is Christianity. Therefore, we believe things contrary to the rest of the world's view.

The world view says homosexuality and other non-heterosexual preferences are okay, it can't be helped or changed, and if you disagree you are hateful and narrowminded, not progressive, backward in your beliefs…this is 2023 after all! We have arrived to enlightenment! Our enlightenment is nothing but darkness that has been around for a long time; however, now it is more acceptable. This is why God is reaching out to mankind, because we have left what He has taught and stands for. We have kicked him out of our lives, school, jobs, government, etc., and wonder why all hell is breaking loose. The Bible says: "My people are destroyed for lack of knowledge" (Hosea 2:6). People just don't know!

I went to university and graduated with a degree in social work (prior to my salvation experience). I am not brilliant, but I am an educated person. I have many years' experience of working in the helping relations profession. I know people and human nature tendencies, etc., pretty well. I've seen some of the messed-up things they go through, what it does and what that makes them believe. I've chased after many things and asked many questions. We all believe in something! God made that void so He could fill it, but we have filled it with everything else.

Sex, fame, money, possessions, drugs, alcohol, sports, whatever thing gets your attention or draws you into your own selfish world. Have you chased after anything? What and why? Even if it's something you don't necessarily consider bad.

This is the sinful and carnal nature that we all struggle with and must put down or it will kill us by separating us from God. If you haven't considered it yet, you must realize that we "walk by faith, not by sight." This is (2 Corinthians 5:7). You cannot be a Christian without faith. It takes faith to believe in Jesus to be your Savior. Likewise, it takes faith to believe that sexual lifestyles that do not line up with God's word are sin.

This is not merely through natural thinking, but rather by the

Spirit of God who brings CONVICTION of sin and revelation knowledge. Conviction of sin is not something that our society really promotes. Quite the contrary, society promotes being your own self. DO what feels good. Basically, be your own God. That's what is wrong with our society today. No parameters as to right and wrong. If it feels good, just do it and enjoy it.

Do you realize that there are some people who are now promoting that the age of consent should be removed and that children should be able to have sex freely with adults? Or should we say so that adults could freely have sex with children! There are words for that, and it's called pedophilia and sexual abuse. It's long been considered outlawed and off limits, but now it's trying to raise its ugly head to be socially accepted. It used to be that sodomy (homosexuality) was outlawed, but now unfortunately this too is socially and legally accepted. Is pedophilia next? Bestiality? God help us. The children have always been the ones abused and used by those caught up in sexual perversion. This has historically always been the demise of declining cultures. The exploitation of children. We have sexual abuse, child pornography and trafficking of children and even child sacrifice! It is rampant, and I'd dare say much more than the average citizen cares to know. Sticking our heads in the sand won't make it disappear. We must take a stand, pray and fight for our children and the future of our society.

As people of God, we should take a Godly stand against what contradicts the Bible. If we don't, we are basically slapping God in the face and saying that His truth doesn't matter to us. If we allow our culture to dictate to us what is acceptable, we will become lost. (Matthew 5:13) reads: "You are the salt of the earth: but if the salt loses its flavor, how shall it be seasoned? It is then good for nothing but to be thrown out and trampled underfoot by men."

We'll get trampled if we take this sitting down. As I've said earlier, I am astounded that anyone calling themselves a Christian would or could agree that homosexuality and other sexual perversions could be a viable lifestyle to live or even support. Gay marriage is NOT allowed in God's word or His Church. Any so-called church that allows a minister to marry same-sex individuals has NO authority to do so by God and is not standing in as a servant of God. Much less the ordaining of such individuals.

Chapter 8
Help

So, what do you do if you or someone you know is struggling with same-sex attractions, etc.? And wants to be set free? And this is the key. One must be convicted that it is a sin worth being set free from! First of all, Jesus is the only one who can help. A person must be born again of the spirit of God. "Jesus answered and said unto him, Verily, verily, I say unto thee, except a man be born again, he cannot see the kingdom of God" (John 3:7).

One MUST be born into the kingdom of light, out of the darkness of sin that we were all born into. This is a supernatural spiritual experience that happens by faith. IF we take possession of the shed blood of Jesus, by faith and His finished work on the cross as a reality, we become a new person. (2 Corinthians 5:17) says: "Therefore, if any man be in Christ, he is a new creature: old things are passed away; behold, all things become new." This is the miracle of Christianity. Our sins are forgiven, and we start a new spiritually charged life journey. Christianity is not a religion with its do's and don'ts, rather it is a relationship that starts with accepting Jesus as Savior and then getting to know Him, His character and ways. A personal relationship forged in the love of God the Father through Jesus Christ. Place your faith in Jesus not only to save you, but to transform (change/convert) you into His likeness.

As I indicated before, it is just your spirit man that is "saved."

You still must deal with your soul: your mind, will and emotions, your flesh as we call it. There are demonic forces and strongholds that we deal with, whether inherited from transgressions, sins or iniquity from ancestors, which result in putting us under a curse. Or just our own demons we have acquired because we have rebelled (sinned) against God or something was perpetrated against us (sexual abuse, rape, molestation, etc.). This opens the door for attack. Demons are real and have authority to inflict harm and havoc on us until we can identify where they have permission to stay and then repent and seek to have them dislodged. I'm talking about spiritual warfare. Growing in Christ. Salvation is just the start of becoming a Christian. You need to get into a good Bible-believing church where the HOLY SPIRIT is recognized and welcomed to minister. Pastors or leaders with an "anointing" to deal with demons is a must if you really want help. Because that is what we are initially dealing with here. There are many churches out there that teach and preach salvation, but don't go much further. You'll have to go deeper in the Spirit to deal with sins such as homosexuality, etc. A PERSON NEEDS DELIVER-ANCE and INNER HEALING. Not all preachers are trained or equipped to deal this way. Some just don't believe in deliverance. Some don't hardly believe in the Devil and his demons as forces that must be resisted and overcome. It's sad, but true. (Mark 16:17): "And these signs will follow those who believe: In my name they will cast out demons, they will speak with new tongues."

Lies, lies, lies. Anyone who believes they are a homosexual or anything else contrary to God's word has succumbed to the belief of a lie from our enemy, Satan. He is the father of lies! The only way to come out of agreement with his lies is to reject it, repent and turn from believing the lie and accept what God says about us. This is the struggle, not only with sexual sin identity, but with any other sinful ways that can affect a person. The word of God can and will renew our thinking. But even then, you must resist the Devil.

(James 4:7): "Submit yourselves therefore to God. Resist the Devil, and he will flee from you." We cannot entertain unclean, unnatural perverse thoughts. Guard your heart and mind. This is difficult as a new Christian because there is so much to sift through, and you'll need to get to know the truth and start living it.

The battle is intense, and a deep-seeded host of issues can contribute to sexual identity confusion, perversion, etc. Parental upbringing, any sort of sexual abuse, pornography, same-sex sexual encounters, and other negative environmental factors can and will influence us.

Society's acceptance of homosexuality as a bonified lifestyle with laws allowing same-sex marriage makes it difficult to fight. A weak or absent father figure and/or overbearing mother figure has often been equated as contributing factors. Again, if a person "feels gay," it may feel as natural to them as those that are not, and you can't convince them otherwise. Only God can do it through the power of the Holy Spirit (the Spirit of truth). (John 16:13): "Howbeit when he, the Spirit of truth, is come, he will guide you into all truth...."

Today there is so much portrayed in the name of "sexual freedom" that a person can easily fall into believing that if others say it is okay and enjoy it, why can't I? It comes down to a choice. Like anything else we have a free will choice in what we believe in this matter. There will be unfortunately those who will reject Christ and therefore continue in homosexuality, etc. Without Christ, they will perish in the end. They will go to Hell. Plain and simple. BUT for someone who accepts Jesus as the Lord, there is hope for change and a new lifestyle and eternal life.

Summary

So, there you have it. My position on sexual perversions of ANY kind. So, what do you think? How has this book affected you and your understanding of this topic? It is not an easy topic to discuss, because it is so charged with personal emotions, feelings and personal experiences. But for anyone truly wanting to understand and be freed from this lifestyle or bondage to sexual confusion and/or addiction, Jesus is the ONLY answer.

I challenge you to take the time to examine what you believe AND why? What is the underlying thought process you are adhering to? How can you help anyone who is caught up in this sin? Well, first they need to accept Christ. You may lead them to Him personally if you know Him or ask God to save them via another avenue if they are not open to discussing salvation with you. Jesus Christ can save anyone. He desires that not one would perish. No one is too far gone. Prayer is paramount. It's not about them acknowledging that their sexuality goes against God's word, but rather that they are a lost sinner and need Jesus.

However, if they claim to be saved, then the Word of God on the matter must be used to show them the error of their thinking and the Holy Spirit must do the convicting. God's word does not return void. Seeking God's will and truth in the matter must be one's goal. Seek and you shall find…. Like earlier stated, one must get involved in a church and/or ministry that has experience with deliverance. Most churches will agree that homosexuality is wrong, but most of them won't be able to minister under the anointing to set the captives free. But it is possible to be set free. Whom the Son has set free is free indeed.

This is the first book I've written. There are others who have authored books on this subject. Please search these out to further supplement your understanding of this complex social and most personal issue. I am hopeful that at least I have opened your eyes, so to speak, to the subject at hand. And have forced you to address your belief system. I continue to grow and gain confidence in who God says I am. I get hit with lies and condemnation like anyone else. I too battle to accept truth, but I do know the truth and his name is JESUS. Regardless of what my flesh tells me, I am a son of God, loved, redeemed and being changed from glory to glory. I won't be perfect until I see Jesus, but I will not accept a lie about myself or anyone else that God somehow creates homosexuals, bisexuals, or transgenders and that it is just the way it is. It is a lie from the pit of HELL to deceive and capture mankind in sin. Plain and simple.

God is GOOD and through the sinful fall of man, Satan has gained inroads into the lives of man and has twisted God's perfect plan for our sexuality. And that is the sexual relationship ONLY between a husband and wife. All else is sin. Including premarital heterosexual sex. Many are guilty of this today and think nothing of it. However, a holy God calls for man to repent of his sins and accept Jesus as Lord.

I would be remiss if I did not thank those who have prayed for me, stood by me, loved me, have laid hands on me and prayed for healing and deliverance at the Lord's bidding. You have been used by God to set this man free and I love and appreciate all of you.

To my lovely, faithful, patient and God-fearing wife, Debbie who has stayed by my side over these 33+ years of marriage, I thank and love you more than you'll ever know. My church family over the years who loved me when I was a mess. I am blessed. Perfect, no, but praising God for what He has brought me through and how He has so greatly loved me through it all. My journey continues, I believe God has great things in store for me and you. I thank you, Lord.

APPENDIX

42

Homosexuality specifically is identified as a perversion in the Bible. Here are some scriptures supporting this:

Old Testament
Gen. 19:1-12
Leviticus 18:22, 20:13
Judges 19:22, 23
1 Kings 14:24
1 Kings 15:12

New Testament
Romans 1:18-32
1 Corinthians 6:9-11
1 Timothy 1:8-10
Jude 5-11

www.ingramcontent.com/pod-product-compliance
Lightning Source LLC
Chambersburg PA
CBHW070325160726